WORDS OF
ENCOURAGEMENT
from my father

JACQUELYN COBB

Brilliant Books Literary
137 Forest Park Lane Thomasville
North Carolina 27360 USA

CONTENTS

DEDICATION

First and foremost, I would like to thank My Lord and Savior, Jesus Christ, for allowing me to tap into his wisdom through the many tests and trials I have endured to make this book come to light. He has been the giver of my words and inspiration to encourage so many people and for that I say, "Thank you Jesus!" I dedicate this book to my family, my devoted husband and friend, Kenneth Cobb, Sr., My beautiful daughters, Brittney Shanea Wright, Charmaine Latrice Sloss (Deceased), my beloved son, Kenneth Maurice Cobb, Jr., my beautiful granddaughters, Kiara Amani Heyward, Kelis Charmaine Seabrook, and Kalyn Alleyiah Bright. Also, I dedicate this book to my loving and caring parents that God blessed me have, whom instilled biblical as well as daily life principles that has equipped me along with The Holy Ghost to weather storms that comes my way, Mr. Robert Lee Wright and Mrs. Irene Wright, whom has gone on to be with The Lord. Last but not least, my siblings, Aisha, Ronald (Deceased), Florence, Edwin, Shane, Jabez, Shone, Tammy, and Carolyn for teaching me how to treat others.

THERE IS HOPE IN JESUS CHRIST

A new day has dawn, the enemy is defeated
No more chaos and pain will be repeated
The atmosphere is bright and full of peace with total victory

Evil is demolished and souls are set free
Jesus defeated the enemy over two thousand years ago
The Holy Ghost is that power that makes all men triumph
Without Jesus Christ, Satan would have won

God, whom is Jesus Christ manifested in the
flesh, allows us to be tested and tried
He knows man wasn't strong enough and
sent his spirit, so man could arise
There is hope in Jesus Christ, our Lord
He expects us to stand together and on one accord
Call on Jesus and plead his blood
The enemy trembles in fear at the mention of his name like a flood
Open your hearts and minds so the spirit of Christ can dwell within
God gives his people the power to resist sin and ultimately win

TALK TO GOD

God is always available to and for us
We need only to pray and in him, put our trust
His answers may be ye, nay or not yet
Pray continually and never fret

Your shoulders become burden less
Cast all of your cares on him, he can handle the stress
Talk to God in sincerity and do it often
He sees your pain and knows when it needs to be soften

Life at times may seem hard, but never give up
Let go and allow God to show you his love
He will give you strength for your weakness
Praying without ceasing and your faith increases

Go to your secret place and meet God there
His abundance in blessings will take away all fear
As you talk to God, he will show you the way
Keep in constant communication with him, so you would not go astray

GIVE GOD YOUR ALL

Don't hold back because the father wants all of you
He blesses your gifts to increase and bring you before many, it's true
Trials come to push us closer to our Father
Jesus's love for you is stronger than any mother

Give God your all and let him enlarge your territory
His spirit will change you and give your life a new story
Jesus paid the ultimate price for your precious soul
Live for him, now and make Heaven your goal

Life changing blessings will be your reward
By faith you will overcome if you keep your trust in The Lord
Never will he leave nor forsake his own
God will make you joint heir and give you a Heavenly home

Give God your all and watch every area of your life prosper
His love will cause you to refuse everything Satan has to offer
Your life is not your own, so don't take it for granted
Trust in God and always serve in gladness

Allow God to be the ruler of your life
He will remove all of your hurt, pain, and strife
Faith will always catch The Lord's attention
He is the only God to conquer death, hell, and the grave's retention

IT'S OKAY TO CRY SOMETIMES

When troubles come, it sometimes causes tears to fall
We are never alone because God is there when we call

Tears can lift heavy burdens as it cleanses the soul
Shedding tears replenishes both the young and old

Holding back tears hurts and doesn't allow healing to start
God's loving presence will calm and soothe any broken heart

All tears are not the result of hurt or pain
We all from time to time shed tears for the joy we sustain

Once you've had a good cry, shake yourself and get back up
Maybe your tears are from receiving so much love

Crying makes one strong and wise at the same time
Why, because a lesson may be learned from a trial sent from the divine

Never be ashamed to shed tears, but be careful whom you trust with your heart
God will show you everything in time so never let his love depart

Our lives aren't always filled with hurt and pain
When you really look at it, shedding tears helps us to stay sane
God promises to help us no matter the situation or time in our lives
He will give us tears of joy so that our souls can continue in him to rise
God Sees it all hiding in the dark will not obstruct The Lord's eyes

GOD SEES IT ALL

He reaches us wherever we may be in life, so don't despise
Holy is God and he can make you flawless
He knows our end form the beginning and delivers us from all distress
God's light dwells in us to make us what he wants us to be
The trials he allows to come in life comes to
make one lean on him dependently
It's true we can do nothing without The Lord's help
Allow him to take away all selfishness and dependability in self
Trials also come to let God show you what you have on the inside
The same results will appear until we give
God the ability to move in our lives
God is omnipresent, sees and knows it all
He loves us so much he will catch us before we fall
The love of God will reach down and pick us up
Prayers will be answered when in him we put our trust

GOD ALWAYS SHOWS
HIMSELF STRONG

Great is the power of God to his Saints
The Lord revives and gives strength to the faint

By his power and might he crushes all of our enemies
His power brings even hypocrites to their knees

God spoke all things into being by his powerful existence
His paths for life will cause one to conquer without resistance

Never will God leave his people in any despair
The abundance of his love shows that he cares

Jesus's blood was shed to give mankind the strength lacked
The power God possesses will cause even his enemies to react

Bodies are healed, the lame walk, all by The Lord's might
Jesus makes unbreakable soldiers to conquer and win every fight

The dead are being raised and tongues confess
That God is real and Lord for all to attest

The Lord has all power in his hand and has proven it through time
He is the author and finisher of our faith that causes men in him to shine

ENDOW MY SOUL WITH FIRE, LORD

Burn away all the things in me Lord that's not like you
Make my soul shine bright as the sun
Oh, how your spirit illuminates my being to bring you all of the glory
Bright is the path you have made for me to walk into

Purify my soul in your word that cultivates your light in me
Take away the stain and the pain that my sins has
caused the beam to cease from radiance
Sincere repentance has opened my blinded eyes to see clearly
Your will is what I want and need to bring all
praises to your holy and righteous name

Dear God, my soul is dim without you in my life
Cancel and destroy all darkness that tries to penetrate your light within
Overshadow the enemy on my behalf because
his desire is to sift me as wheat
Anoint every part of my being to be as transparent as you

When you look at me you see me as I will be and nothing less
Because you will never leave nor forsake me, others can see who you are
My soul is yearning for your touch that will make me new again
Endow my soul with fire, Lord until no glimpse of sin will be there

JESUS CHRIST IS LORD

Souls are saved and lives are changed
Forgiveness of sin is given if repentance is sincere in Jesus name

Diseases and sickness must leave the souls of men souls
Death is defeated because God is yet in control

Storms of life are turned by The Lord's mighty and strong hand
The scriptures, which are food for the soul, were given to help one to stand

Souls are saved from all hurt, pain, and destruction
The Holy Ghost was sent to share with man God's word with an unction

Jesus Christ is super and has the power to give one rest
He doesn't need a red cape or the letter S on his chest

Never will there be another Savior as he
Jesus Christ gave his life for all souls to be free

Power is in the hand God of the Maker of all
Living for him causes all men in the spirit to stand tall

Jesus Christ gives to all the things that are sown
Jesus Christ is Lord of all and his word is health and nourishment for
the bone

WE MUST LOVE EACH OTHER

If God looks beyond our flaws and weaknesses
Who are we not to let our love through him not to increase
The Lord commanded us to love is spite of color,
class, status, background, and such
God shows us who he is by his genuine love
Falling short of God's Glory has every man committed on earth
God loves us enough to look beyond our fault,
flaws, and sins, but, yet sees our worth
The Lord's love has the power to melt the hardest of hearts
Genuine love like the love of The Father is
what sets his chosen people apart
Love covers a multitude of sin, according to the
scriptures, because all have sinned
We must love each other and reach out to help others to win
If we see our brothers and sisters sins, we ought to lift them up in prayer
God sits high and looks low, but see the hearts
of men to see if they genuinely care
We must love those whom may be at times unlovable
All go through tests and trials that will cause pain and struggle
We must love each other because it is good and right
Showing love is fulfilling the scriptures that was
given by our Lord and Savior, Jesus Christ

THE PRINCE OF PEACE

My Savior brings calm to all of my storms
He gives me strength when I am weak and torn

Jesus gives us peace that passes all understanding in him
The Lord directs our paths that guarantees that we will win

Serenity is what The Prince of Peace gives
God is his word and helps all who receive him to freely live

The Lord comforts all to walk in obedience because it's the right way
Jesus quickens men spirits with confidence when they pray

The meditation on God's agape love opens the heart of man
When one feels the pain of loss, Jesus shows him how to stand

To be entangled in Christ brings a calm refreshing
God gives us patience during the time of testing

Oh, Prince of Peace, I need you to be near
Your spirit blankets me when my enemies come to destroy me in fear

GOD, THE DELIVERER
OF MY SOUL

Whatever comes my way, God is there
If I fail, The Lord lets me know he cares
When I am down, Jesus lifts me up
If friends turn away, God shows me his enormous love

My soul can rest in the arms of my Savior
He blesses me with honor and favor
Christ paid for my soul with his blood in full
My enemies are defeated as I stand still

If my light gets dim from sin, God overshadows me with his light
I cast all of my cares on him to make all things right
When my strength is weak, God gives me his joy
If my enemies strike, my God will destroy

Oh, my soul is anchored in Jesus's grace
My redeemer is near to help me finish this race
No longer am I bound to this evil world's plot
I am victorious because all of my battles are
won by my Savior on the spot

I AM A WINNER IN GOD

All of my enemies are defeated in Jesus name
They fell in their plots, schemes, and games
My God always fights and defends me
Now I am winning and walking in victory

The weapons of all my enemies did form
But Didn't prosper because my God still sits on his throne
I refuse to walk in fear, torment or shame
Because of Jesus, I have conquered death and I am without blame

A winner through Jesus is what I am
Victory is so sweet so, boldly I stand
My enemies are now under my feet
Now, holding their heads down in total defeat

Conquered all of the very ones whom have caused me pain and hurt
Now, they back away exposed by their deeds and dirt
Hallelujah, I have won the battle because the Lord showed me how to fight
God made all of my enemies footstools and has thrust them out of my sight

WELL DONE

Walking upright with Jesus in love aluminates his praise
Expressions of The Lord's love causes me to walk in his ways
Leaving all darkness behind to shine oh so bright
Living an abundant life entangled in Jesus Christ
Depending on God and the promises of his word alone
Overcoming the temptations because my Savior still sits on his throne
Never ever giving up because God is always there
Entering life eternally with Jesus is why death can't cause me no fear

THE LORD IS THE GOD
OF ABUNDANCE

Freely will God bless and it's always more than enough

His love is unconditional and never wavers

The Lord is faithful as long as you put your trust in him

Your faults he looks beyond to meet your need

Blessings overtake those whom remain faithful unto his word

God's hand is mighty and moves mountains to reach you where you are

He justifies those he has chosen and call to do his work and far greater

The judgements of our Heavenly Father is just because he is so patient with us

Jesus purifies by the trials and tests he allows or sends to take away all impurities

A vessel of honor is what he will make the one who is obedient and willing

The Prince of Peace sends the comforter, the Holy Ghost, to lead and direct your path

The wisdom of his anointing will destroy all of your enemies that come up against you

When we fall short he is our advocate that intercedes when the enemy accuses

JUST BECAUSE

Just because life throws stress your way, God steps in quick
The Lord knows you can bear this test, so pray and never give in or quit
Changes come in the most difficult times
because being tried by fire purifies
God knows everything and nothing catches him off guard or surprise

Just because others gave up on you or walked out
doesn't mean God has forgotten you
Life is a gift purchased by his own blood for your salvation, it's true
Jesus gives the test to give us a testimony to tell others of his goodness
Joy comes in the nick of time to relieve you from all distress

Just because the world turn their backs on you don't
mean it wasn't apart of The Lord's plan
Our life is already mapped out to give God
all of the glory, do you understand
Remember if he brought you out before, it will
never be difficult for The Lord to do again
Jesus is the mind regulator who steps in your trials
when the enemy tries to make you insane

I PUT MY TRUST IN YOU GOD

If darkness is all around, I depend on you
Temptations on every hand, you come to my rescue

When my vision is not clear, you guide me through
Even when I fail, you stand as my advocate defending me, too

While the enemy is trying to deceive, you boldly show up
When it seems no one cares, you show me tremendous love

On my low days, you send your light to shine from above
The Holy Spirit brings all things to my remembrance and rests on me
like a dove

Lord in you I will put my trust
Its's my honor to tell others being born-again is a must

Your spirit changed my life of sin into a life of living just
In spite of my wrong, you continue to meet my needs without a fuss

When my enemies surrounds me, you break them with fear
God you encourage me and that you truly care

Your spirit focuses my spiritual vision so that I see everything so clear
I trust you Lord to answer me every one of my earnest prayers

DEPRESSION IS DEFEATED

If you are in need of deliverance from depression, trust
God Let him give you a life of a new start
Obey his word and be filled with joy and strength
Jesus wants to save you from the sadness
and will go through great lengths
Feelings of guilt and worthlessness will have to go
The word of God will nourish your mind
and help you to continue to grow
Depression is sadness sent form Satan, your soul's enemy
One touch from The Lord will put your mind at ease
I decree laughter and joy will be apart of your life
I declare healing from all pain and strife
God gives the gift of The Holy Ghost to give power to the faint
Come to Jesus as you are and sincerely repent
God will never ever let go of your hand
His anointing will allow you to boldly stand
Depression in your life, God will help you to overcome
You will hold your head up high because with
Jesus the victory is already won

LIFE'S STRUGGLES
BRINGS STRENGTH

Hard times come, but don't last long
Trials causes one to become better and strong
Criticism comes from the ones close to you whom you trust
Misunderstanding causes a lot of confusion and disgust

God allows tests to come to build your faith
He shows up in trying times just for our sake
Trust in the Lord and he will make the trials of none effect, small
His love in our hearts keeps us in line and is there if we fall

God's light shines in our life when it's blinding and dark
His spirit brings peace to our minds as well as our hearts
Never will our Savior leave us completely alone
The blood of Jesus cleanses and makes our sins be atoned

Heartache and pain brings out the best in us
Like gold being purified by fire in him we should put our trust
Misfortune brings tears and sometimes lots of hurt
Yet, it comes about to teach that we should always put God first

Lessons are learned and tests are graciously passed
One is given insight for a life time that will last
Experience doesn't always have to be one's teacher
Some may learn from the mistakes of others or hear it from a preacher

DENOUNCING MY ENEMY

You tried to destroy me because of jealousy
But God is my strength, now I walk in victory
Mocking and talking about me to all
Now, your mocking only makes me stand tall

You never was a positive person in my life
All you have caused me was pain and strife
Your soul is at the brink of hell's fire
Time's up for you and it's looking pretty dire

Never will you see victory against me gain
God has defeated you in my life my so called friend
Scandalous was your life here on earth
Burn now and forever my friend, you are cursed

Enraged are you because you want things your way
All of this you've caused me has reversed and now it's time to pay
The final resting place is heated just for people like you
You've made your bed in hell and now deal with
my God because you are doomed

LORD, I NEED YOUR STRENGTH

Oh, Lord you are so valiant and unbreakable
The Holy Ghost within me is incredible

Without your strength, I won't make it
Endow me with your strength Lord, every bit

Lord, your strength has such massive power
Oh, how I need you to overtake me every second, minute, and hour

Without your anointing, I will ultimately fall
I know you will answer every time you hear my earnest call

Lord, I need your strength to make me whole
Let your glorious power quench my soul

Your strength make me spiritually strong and bold
No other display of power has ever been told

God, you alone fulfilled my life, it's true
Though I fail at times, you still see me through

Your power gives me all that I really need
Thank you Lord for your power dwelling in me

FAITH TO MOVE MOUNTAINS

Believe you can achieve and God will make it happen
Pray with expectancy and never stop asking
Faith in God is key and a very powerful thing
His spirit has power like an eagle's wings

Mountains will fall as long as you keep the faith
The Lord gives us power to decree things every single day
Speak to life's issues that come to weigh you down
God's strength can make your mountains that seem high drown

Trust God to do the impossible
No situation in your life is and unsolvable obstacle
The Lord gives us power to victoriously rise
Keep him in your focus always because he holds in his hands your prize

BECAUSE OF YOU

Life in you is now complete
Never will your people suffer defeat
Our soul has a hiding place
Because of you, Lord, many walk in faith

The stain from sin has been lifted
You've endowed us with the power in your midst
Through you, tribulation is made small
Because of you, Jesus, we give you our all

Calvary bore all of our nasty sins
We walk in victory because you live within
Tragedy, heartache, and all types of evil has failed
Because of you, God, love will only prevail

Oh, how our plights will ultimately bring change
All of the enemy's plans fail again and again
Walking in favor, you gave us the authority
Because of you, Great I AM, our souls live in tranquility

You chose us to become fishers of men
Souls cry out to you, a true friend
The sick healed and the dumb speak
Because of blood the enemy has to flee

I APOLOGIZE

Please forgive me for all the pain I have caused
Lord, don't let my foolishness cause precious souls to be lost
Help me dear Lord to also forgive myself
The thought of my sins displeasing you hinders my health and wealth
Please continue to place my faults in the sea of forgiveness
I give you all of the praise and myself to take away the unneeded stress
Help me to do the things that are pleasing in your sight
Open up my understanding so that I will do only what is right
Never let me fall to the point that I can't get back up
Lord, forgive me for not walking and trusting in you, love
Thank you for forgiveness because I know that you are merciful
Guide me my Savior and tell me when I must stand still

WHO IS GOD

John 1:1-14 reveals that you yet live
God you are the word and the spirit of love that gives
You became flesh and walk among men
Proving your holy deity in boldness and called us friend

You are Jesus Christ, The Holy One
Our risen Savior whom is the giver of life and challenged death and won
The light that lights every woman, girl, boy, and man
The holder of the world and everything within with your mighty hands

Jesus Christ and God whom are one and the same
Our advocate when we fall and when the enemy wants to blame
Agape love whom loves unconditionally and without measure
The creator of heaven and earth that show what to treasure

The name that is above every name ever in existence
A protector whom will come to the rescue in spite of distance
Tempted you were, but without sin
Conqueror of death, hell, and the grave whom is the example to show us
how to win

WONDERFUL COUNSELOR

Oh, how great and wise you are
Always directing me and making ways by far
You understand and know my every move and thought
Making sure my motive and attitude are right without plot
Your wisdom opens my eyes as my footsteps are being guided
Your counsel is beyond measure and you never ever hide it
A wonderful counselor whom made me over
with strength, wisdom, and favor
Filled with understanding and knowledge for all to savor
Giver of testimonies to encourage souls that need an encouraging word
Lord, you are unlike any other god on earth that we have heard

YOUR LOVE GIVES ME STRENGTH

My love for you has grown from all of my life's trials
Oh, how you care for me because I am your child
What can I say?
Your love gives me strength to please you
It gives me the unction to do the things I need to do
Can you see the love I have for you in my heart?
I never ever want your love in my life to depart

Your love gives me the strength I've never had
It lifts me up every time I am afraid or sad
What can I say?
The love you give make me want to continue to live
My love for you is why I give of myself when you tell me to give
Oh, the love in my heart comes from you and will never die
It gives me courage to move forward and continue to try

THERE IS A GOD

Catastrophe tries to put fear in all
But the glory of God always stands tall
The sky changes from gray to blue
The sun shines to give a clear view
Birds fly high as the wind puts them to the test
God displays his majesty for all to attest
Creation is God's canvas on Heaven's easel
God spreads his love by using people
Trees gives us what we need from the crisp air
Rain ceases so the sun can reappear
How do these things take place, do you know?
There is a God and he is in full control

THE TIME IS NOW

Get your spiritual house in order
God is soon to return for his own
He has given all men time to make things right
Give yourselves to him while you have breath
God can change the most hideous sinner
The Lord forgives all who sincerely asks
Don't waste any more time because he is soon to appear
Jesus Christ took our place at Calvary's cross
He gives us all free will and not forces us to serve
All souls that turn a deaf ear will be at risk
Serve God now because the excuses will be unaccepted

SALVATION IS FREE

Al souls need Jesus Christ
The Alpha and Omega, he is the giver of life
Love is his nature and he forgives all sins
Awesome is the Lord and Savior
Triumphant in all his way, oh what splendor
Imaged us as he is, a father to all
Omnipotent, beautiful, and stands tall
New mercies he gives to us all everyday
Increases our faith in him always
Sovereign God who gave his life
Freedom he gives to those whom lives right
Redeemer of mankind is what he is
Excellent in mercy and quick to forgive
Exalted high above all, He is God our king
Ruler of nations and truth, my Savior conquers everything

GIVE GOD A TRY

Our maker desires to bless us inside and out
Bless his name, give him love, or sound off in a shout
The Lord heals all diseases of all whom have a sick sin soul
No respect of person he blesses both the young and old
Falling short everyday proves that we are in need of God
His yoke is easy and he gives us his spirit to live a life that isn't hard
Our faith in him makes him move on our behalf
Only what we do for Christ will ultimately last
Praise God in and out of season
Lift his name up his for any reason
Jesus is standing by to hear your call
He will be there always especially if you should fall
Give God a try so you can walk in the newness of life
He will deliver you from darkness and bring you into his marvelous light

FIRE AND BRIMSTONE

Hot is the fire that burns in hell
Unquenchable it is and made for those who rebel
Brimstone will fall from the sky above
It scars the souls, leaving them gnashing their
teeth with emptiness and no love
Disobedient souls will dwell forever in the bottomless pit
The Pharisees and hypocrites will be the ultimate fit
Time is of the essence to turn far away from sin
There will be no excuse on judgement day where punishment will begin

LOOK WHAT JESUS HAS DONE

Mocked, beaten, and crucified is what Jesus has done
He was the greatest example to show mankind how living holy declares
he has won
Defeated death, hell, and the grave, Jesus made it all possible
We too can be victorious because he specializes in the impossible
Our Savior showed us that faith can move the mountains that seem hard
in our lives
Jesus still sits high on his throne because he has risen and yet alive
He fed five-thousand souls with just one prayer
He also healed the sick, raised the dead, and caused the deaf to hear
The Lord turned water into wine and defeated all demons and devils
Casted evil spirits out of lost souls and walked on water in spite of the level
All these thing and more did The Prince of peace has done
Many will stand in awe when he returns for his daughters and sons

GOD'S FAVOR

The favor of God is wonderful and cannot be compared to no other
His favor blesses those whom are righteous and
faithful without unrepented sins covered
The favor of The Lord makes the things that
seems impossible come to light
Though man may fall, God looks beyond it
and blesses with all of his might
Even during life's testing periods, God will allow
his favor to bring us victoriously out
The overflow of his favor will put a song in
our hearts or makes one shout
Sometimes it may seem that favor isn't fair
to those whom don't understand
What one must realize is that God is the one
who gives favor and it is in his hands
God's favor will take one from the bottom and put him at the top
He favors those whom he chooses not because
his favor cannot be bought
His favor is rewarded without measure to
those who will believe and receive
God tries the hearts of men and gives favor ever so abundantly

JESUS IS ALWAYS THERE

Jesus is always there whether times are bad or good
Even when one falls and doesn't do what he or she could
While in the mountain top or down in the valley
When demons try to discourage to make one unhappy
All alone and seems no one cares
Jesus promises to always be there
In sunshine or inclement weather
He promises to always be there
Either in death or in life
Pain or strife
Jesus will make everything alright
He promises to stick closer than a brother
Shows his love alike that of a mother
God will never leave us or forsake us
Especially if he is the only one whom we put our trust
Call on him because he is just a breath away
Jesus knows it all even if you don't have the words to say
Trust in him because he keeps his word
He will prove himself over and over in spite of what you have heard

ALL SOULS ARE PRECIOUS
TO CHRIST

If you are born again or an unbeliever, Christ cares for you
He will show you that there is nothing to big or small for him to do
Your soul is the apple of his eyes
So, humble yourself and give Christ Jesus a try
Whether backslidden or ignorant to his being, The Lord will love you, too
To that one whom is depressed or strung out on drugs
Allow Christ to shower you with his unconditional love
Christ has no pleasure in seeing a soul dying in their sins
He came to show mankind that in him they too can win
Never will another love precious souls like this
Christ gave his life for all and was beaten for it and whipped
He shed his blood on the cross
Because he didn't want anyone's soul to be lost

A LOVE LIKE GOD'S

Unconditional and oh so sweet
Blows my mind and sweeps me off of my feet
Gives me strength to mount up like eagles
Lifts me up and keeps my heart strong and real

Moves mountains my enemies have set
Keeps away all things to regret
Makes my soul leap with constant joyfulness
Reminds me that in him, I am blessed

More than the whole entire world against me
Takes away all of my doubts and sets my soul free
Gave his life so that my own can be saved
Rose to Glory, now all of the world raves

Will receive me as his own one day
Keeps my mind, so I won't go astrayBurns in my soul so deep within
Forgiver of all of my terrible and disgusting sins

GOD HAS ALL POWER

Their is nothing too hard for my God to do
Mighty is he that gave his life for every people and multitude
Oh, the power of God makes every demon tremble
Their is no other god whose power resembles

The dead are being raised
Debts and all bills are being canceled and paid
The dumb has the ability to speak
Souls that are bound are being set free

Sick bodies are healed and made whole
Prophesy is being revealed to both the young and old
Demons are cast out of tormented souls
The strength God gives make the timid bold

Souls are being nourished all by his word
The gospel is still changing lives, haven't you heard
The lame limbs are being strengthened as they graciously walk
Death is overcome by the power of God's flock

Limbs grow back to their perfect size
The dead in Christ will soon get up and rise
The return of Jesus Christ is oh so near
All men will overcome if they are faithful without fear

THE ALMIGHTY ONE

Oh, how great is God
His strength is fierce and without measure
Mighty is The Lord's right hand
The enemy is defeated and is cast into outer darkness

With one touch, bodies are healed
God's voice speaks all things that exists
Sin-sick souls are delivered from the grip of death
The Gospel of Jesus Christ is spread abroad

Angels bow down all day and night in awe
Men souls praise God and his marvelous majesty
Awesome is The Great I Am
Hallelujah to the lover of all men souls

God sits high and sees everything upon his vast throne
Sending down blessings after trials of life and passed tests
Wonderful is the name of Jesus Christ
What a Prince and he is forever reverenced

The precious blood Jesus shed was not in vain
His glory surpasses any of the enemy travesties
Oh, how powerful is The Lord, Jesus Christ
High and lifted up in all of his might

IF GOD BE FOR ME

I don't have to fear
The Lord will always be near
God promised me that he will never ever leave me
His promises are sure, so I trust and believe
I stand on God's word because it is life
It helps me to grow and also live right
Fear is all gone and I've got the victory
Triumphant through Jesus Christ, I will always be
God is for me and he never fails
He defeated all of my enemies and in him I prevail
The Lord of host is my sun that shines so bright
He is my victor in every spiritual fight
The God of glory is the lifter of my head
He is my warm pillow as I lay asleep in bed
Oh, how I love my Jesus so
He cleanses my soul from my head to my toes
God has shown me his abundant love
Forever my God reigns high above
Jesus is the giver of life, peace, and grace
Oh, how it will be when I see my Savior face to face

DRUNKEN BY THE HOLY SPIRIT

Oh, a feeling and change has came over me
A spirit of freedom and unending liberty
This spirit not only came over me, but took full control
But it dwells on the inside of me with an evidence of an outward glow
When I walk in the spirit, It takes me off of my feet
It makes me cry tears of joy every time I seek
God and his purpose will be revealed through me, his being
Drunk in the spirit of love gives me meaning
This is no ordinary drunkenness that I feel
God placed his spirit deep within and it is oh so real
Healed from the hand of all my enemies
I have no need to stay bound because Jesus came and set me free
Drunken by the Holy Spirit, not of strong drink
It lifts me up high every time I start to sink

www.ingramcontent.com/pod-product-compliance
Lightning Source LLC
Chambersburg PA
CBHW020346130626
46549CB00003B/1318